Are You PC?

101 Questions to Determine if You are Politically Correct

By the PC Committee

Ten Speed Press
Berkeley, California

Copyright © 1991 by the PC Committee.

All rights reserved. No part of this book
may be reproduced in any form,
except for the purpose of brief reviews,
without the written permission of the publisher.

Ten Speed Press
Box 7123
Berkeley, CA 94707

Text design by the text design committee
Cover design by the cover design committee
Editorial work done by the editorial committee
Illustrations selected by the illustrative committee
Printing and binding scheduled by the
printing and binding collective

Library of Congress Cataloging-in-Publication Data

Are you PC? / by the PC Committee.
    p.   cm.
ISBN 0-89815-447-2
1. Politics—Humor. 2. Questions and answers.
    I. PC Committee (U.S.)
PN6231.P6A63   1991
320'.0207—dc20   91-22370
                                             CIP

First Printing, 1991
Printed in the United States of America

2 3 4 5 — 95 94 93 92 91

CONTENTS

INTRODUCTION

Are You PC?" is an exercise in subjectivity—no one answer is correct. The object is to answer each question as honestly as you can.

Scoring: The most politically correct answer to each question receives the most points; the least politically correct answer receives none. Thus, your score decreases as you get less politically correct. The two questions addressed specifically to women are offset in the final tally by two questions specifically addressed to men.

After finishing the quiz, consult the PC Scale for an interpretation of your total score. Scoresheets are located in the Appendix along with the PC Glossary. Note: The scoring system and the PC Scale are based strictly on the opinions of the PC Committee, so, by definition, they are completely biased.

PC SPEAK

Are you linguistically correct? Do you know which words are considered taboo by PC standards? The following quiz will enlighten you.

PC Speak   **QUESTION #1**

What does the term "PC" make you think of?

- (3)   Politically correct
- (2)   Personal computer
- (1)   Petty cash
- (0)   Police car

PC Speak   **QUESTION #2**

Of the following four choices, which do you use most in conversation?

- (3)   Animal companion
- (2)   My dog (cat, etc.)
- (1)   Pet
- (0)   Laboratory bait

PC Speak   QUESTION #3

Of the following four choices, which do you use most often in conversation?

- (3)   Differently sized
- (2)   Overweight
- (1)   Fat
- (0)   Tub of lard

PC Speak   QUESTION #4

Of the following four choices, which do you use most often in conversation?

- (3)   Differently sized
- (2)   Undersized
- (1)   Short
- (0)   Dwarf

PC Speak　QUESTION #5

Of the following four choices, which do you use most often in conversation?

- (3) Physically challenged or Differently abled
- (2) Disabled
- (1) Handicapped
- (0) Crippled

PC Speak　QUESTION #6

Of the following four choices, which do you use most often in conversation?

- (3) Temporarily abled
- (2) Able-bodied
- (1) Healthy
- (0) Normal

PC Speak　QUESTION #7

Of the following four choices, which do you use most often in conversation?

- (3) Hearing-impaired
- (2) Hard of hearing
- (1) Deaf
- (0) Deaf as a doorknob

PC Speak QUESTION #8

Of the following four choices, which do you use most often in conversation?

    (3)   Speech impaired
    (2)   Nonverbal
    (1)   Mute
    (0)   Dumb

PC Speak QUESTION #9

Of the following four choices, which do you use most often in conversation?

    (3)   Visually impaired
    (2)   Sightless
    (1)   Blind
    (0)   Blind as a bat

PC Speak QUESTION #10

Of the following four choices, which do you use most often in conversation?

    (3)   Developmentally delayed
    (2)   A little slow
    (1)   Mentally retarded
    (0)   Brain damaged

PC Speak   QUESTION #11

Of the following four choices, which do you use most often in conversation?

    (3)   Emotionally disturbed
    (2)   Mentally ill
    (1)   Deranged
    (0)   Wacko

PC Speak   QUESTION #12

Of the following four choices, which do you use most often in conversation?

    (3)   Euro-American
    (2)   Caucasian
    (1)   White
    (0)   Whitebread

PC Speak   QUESTION #13

Of the following four choices, which do you use most often in conversation?

    (3)   Person of Color
    (2)   Nonwhite
    (1)   Black
    (0)   Colored

PC Speak QUESTION #14

How many of the following phrases do you use in everyday conversation? (a) African-American instead of Black (b) Indian American instead of Indian (c) Latino/Latina instead of Hispanic (d) Asian-American instead of Oriental

- (3) All three
- (2) Two
- (1) One
- (0) None

PC Speak QUESTION #15

How many of the following phrases do you use in everyday conversation? (score one point for each answer)

- (1) Humankind instead of mankind
- (1) Postal worker instead of mailman
- (1) People power instead of manpower
- (1) Ovular instead of seminar

PC Speak QUESTION #16

How many of the following phrases do you use in conversation? (score one point for each answer)

- (1) Gay instead of Homosexual Male
- (1) Lesbian instead of Homosexual Female
- (1) Outing instead of Homosexual Celebrity Gossip
- (1) Homophobia instead of Homosexual Oppression

PC Speak   QUESTION #17

How many of the following phrases do you use in everyday conversation? (a) a chink in the armor (b) a nip in the air (c) calling a spade a spade.

- (3) None—because they contain words that have been used in the context of prejudice.
- (2) One
- (1) Two
- (0) All three

PC Speak   QUESTION #18

How many of the following terms do you use in everyday conversation? (a) Dutch treat (b) to Gyp (c) to Jew

- (3) None, because they reinforce cultural stereotypes
- (2) One
- (1) Two
- (0) All three

PC Speak   QUESTION #19

Of the following four choices, which do you use most often in conversation?

- (3) Senior citizen
- (2) Elderly
- (1) Mature
- (0) Old fart

QUESTION #20

Of the following four choices, which do you use most often in conversation?

- (3) Pre-women
- (2) Young women
- (1) Teenage girls
- (0) Jailbait

PC ATTITUDES

The following quiz is a litmus test of your PC quotient. A simple yes or no will do.

PC Attitudes   QUESTION #21

Do you believe that every test is inherently culturally biased?

     (1)   Yes
     (0)   No

PC Attitudes   QUESTION #22

Do you make sure to buy only "cruelty-free" products?

     (1)   Yes
     (0)   No

PC Attitudes   QUESTION #23

Do you find fur coats offensive?

     (1)   Yes
     (0)   No

QUESTION #24

Do you eat only "dolphin safe" tuna?

- (1) Yes
- (0) No

QUESTION #25

Would you accept reduced profits from your investments rather than invest in companies with policies that you find improper?

- (1) Yes
- (0) No

QUESTION #26

Do you believe that every person is racist?

- (1) Yes
- (0) No

QUESTION #27

Do you refer to "non-physically challenged" people as "temporarily able-bodied?"

- (1) Yes
- (0) No

QUESTION #28

Have you been to a "scent-free" event?

- (1) Yes
- (0) No

Are you a vegetarian for moral reasons?

- (1) Yes
- (0) No

Have you checked to see if this book was printed on recycled paper?

- (1) Yes
- (0) No

Have you smiled at least once since picking up this book?

- (1) No
- (0) Yes

STEREOTYPES

Your reaction to stereotypes is a sure sign of PC sensitivity. Pick the response that most closely matches your response to the following encounters.

QUESTION #32

What is your first impression of a person in a military uniform?

- (3) Somebody forced to become an institutionalized killer out of economic necessity.
- (2) A volunteer for violence.
- (1) A patriot.
- (0) Somebody willing to kick ass for Uncle Sam.

QUESTION #33

What is your first impression of a homeless person asking for spare change?

- (3) I get angry at the system for ignoring those most inneed.
- (2) It saddens me to see someone in that condition.
- (1) I would avoid them since they are probably mentally ill.
- (0) Why should I subsidize their drug habit?

Stereotypes QUESTION #34

What is your first impression of a suspect being physically restrained by a police officer?

- (3) It's just another act of police brutality.
- (2) Everybody is innocent until proven guilty.
- (1) I'm glad the police are protecting me from criminals.
- (0) Extremism in the defense of liberty is no vice.

Stereotypes QUESTION #35

What is your first impression of an extremely overweight person?

- (3) I take no special notice of the differently sized.
- (2) I'm glad I'm not that fat.
- (1) Is it genetic or do they lack control?
- (0) They should consider radical liposuction.

Stereotypes QUESTION #36

What is your first impression of a gay couple engaging in a public display of affection?

- (3) Same sex couples are no different than heterosexual couples. Therefore, I would pay no attention.
- (2) I might notice but I would not act differently.
- (1) I dislike people flaunting their sexuality in public, particularly homosexuals.
- (0) I would publicly display my disgust.

Stereotypes　　QUESTION #37

What is your first impression of a rock video featuring scantily clad women?

    (3)   I think of the harmful effects of objectifying women in a sexist culture.

    (2)   I think of it as a sleazy but laughable attempt to cash in on sex-crazed teenage boys.

    (1)   It is symbolic of the decadence and loose morals that were introduced in the 60s.

    (0)   Awwwwright!

Stereotypes   QUESTION #38

An underage pregnant woman?

- (3) It would be ageism to pass judgment— she's like any other pregnant woman.
- (2) She is a symbol of our failure to provide sex education to our nation's youth.
- (1) She is a symbol of loose morals and the disintegration of the American family.
- (0) Sterilize her.

Stereotypes   QUESTION #39

A young African-American male driving a fancy sportscar?

- (3) Any judgment would be racist.
- (2) How people choose to spend their money is their business.
- (1) I question his priorities and wonder how a young person, regardless of race, could afford such luxury.
- (0) Either he's a drug dealer or the car is hot.

QUESTION #40

What is your first impression of a middle-aged caucasian man driving a fancy sportscar?

    (3)   A member of the privileged class reaping the rewards of being white and male in a racist, sexist, capitalist system and narcissistically consuming precious energy sources.

    (2)   How people choose to spend their money is their business.

    (1)   Someone living the American dream.

    (0)   I wonder if my car can dust his.

PC ISSUES

This section of the quiz touches on the major PC issues of our time including racism, sexism, environmentalism, multiculturalism, patriotism, and militarism. They are presented in alphabetical order to avoid favoritism.

Ableism   QUESTION #41

You are feeling ill, so you drive to the pharmacy to pick up some medication. All the spaces close to the entrance are taken. Do you park in an open handicapped parking space?

(3) The correct phrase is disabled parking spot. Or differently abled parking spot. Or physically challenged parking spot. And the answer is no.

(2) Yes, but I only if I really didn't feel well.

(1) Yes, if I am temporarily able.

(0) Yes. I normally park there anyway.

Ageism QUESTION #42

Do you agree with the adage "life begins at 40"?

  (3) No. The quality of one's life is not contingent upon one's age.

  (2) I used to say "never trust anybody over 30," but now I recognize this statement as an indiscretion made by the temporarily young.

  (1) It doesn't sound logical. After all, your odds of dying increase each year.

  (0) I agree with the adage "live fast, die young, and leave a good-looking corpse."

Animal Rights QUESTION #43

If you won a fur coat on a TV game show, what would you do?

  (3) I don't even own a television.

  (2) I would sell the fur and donate the money to an animal rights group.

  (1) I would give it to someone who wanted it.

  (0) I would jump up and down, kiss the emcee and scream "Oh, it's just what I always wanted!"

QUESTION #44

If your home was infested with mice, what would you do to get rid of them?

- (3) I would call the ASPCA.
- (2) I would use a humane mouse trap and set them free in a proper environment.
- (1) I would use any method that worked—including poison or mousetraps—to get rid of them.
- (0) I'd stop feeding the cat.

QUESTION #45

Do you think that it is moral to test a potential cure for cancer on mammals such as white mice and monkeys?

- (3) No. Since animals experience pain just like humans do, all animal testing is cruel and immoral.
- (2) I don't feel it's right but sometimes it's the only way medical progress can be made. Researchers should make sure to avoid causing any unnecessary pain.
- (1) Morals have nothing to do with it. Animals don't understand pain the way humans do. Would you rather have humans suffering?
- (0) Sounds moral to me; after all, when they find a cure, all those little white mice with cancer can be cured.

Censorship   QUESTION #46

Should the government cut funding to controversial artists?

    (3)   No. The government is in no position to judge art. Funding cuts are a blatant attempt to silence artists who do not conform to mainstream values.

    (2)   No. Many works of art that are now considered masterpieces were controversial or misunderstood in their time.

    (1)   The government should support art, but not pornography.

    (0)   Who needs art when we have television?

Environmentalism   QUESTION #47

Which of the following best describes your philosophy on energy conservation?

    (3)   We owe it not only to ourselves but to future generations to save our planet's resources.

    (2)   I want to reduce our dependence on foreign oil.

    (1)   I like the lower utility bills.

    (0)   Why should I restrict my energy consumption when, thanks to nuclear power, our energy sources are infinite.

Environmentalism   QUESTION #48

How do you carry your groceries home?

- (3) In a natural-fiber cloth bag that I bring to the store.
- (2) I ask for paper bags which I later recycle.
- (1) I ask for paper inside plastic.
- (0) I ask for plastic inside plastic.

Environmentalism   QUESTION #49

What type of container do you use when buying a beverage to go?

- (3) I carry my own mug wherever I go.
- (2) I insist on a cup made of biodegradable products before I'll buy it.
- (1) I take whatever is handed to me.
- (0) I ask for Styrofoam.

Environmentalism   QUESTION #50

How many of the following steps have you taken to prevent the destruction of the rainforest? (score one point for each answer)

- (1) I avoid buying furniture made of tropical hardwood.
- (1) I avoid using disposable wooden chopsticks made from tropical hardwood.
- (1) I bought a T-shirt from the Rainforest Action Network.
- (1) I eat Ben and Jerry's "Rainforest Crunch" ice cream.

Environmentalism QUESTION #51

How many of the following steps have you taken to conserve water?

- (1) I shut off the water while brushing my teeth.
- (1) I installed a low-flow shower head.
- (1) I bathe less frequently.
- (1) I flush the toilet less often.

Environmentalism QUESTION #52

Which of the following steps have you taken to prevent the depletion of the ozone layer, global warming, and the greenhouse effect?

- (1) I drive less.
- (1) I avoid all aerosol sprays.
- (1) I planted a tree to reduce carbon dioxide levels.
- (1) I switched to roll-on deodorant.

Environmentalism QUESTION #53

A person drops a candy wrapper in front of you. How do your react?

- (3) I would take immediate action and demand that the offender pick up the trash.
- (2) I would pick it up myself and say nothing.
- (1) I would pick it up if it didn't look too dirty.
- (0) I probably wouldn't notice.

Health Issues QUESTION #54

How should society prevent the spread of sexually transmitted diseases?

- (3) Distribute free condoms and hypodermic needles.
- (2) Encourage safe sex.
- (1) Encourage monogamy.
- (0) Lower the cost of 900 telephone numbers.

Health Issues QUESTION #55

How do you feel about red meat consumption?

- (3) I don't eat it for moral reasons—it is inhumane, hurts the environment, and is no longer necessary for meeting one's nutritional needs.
- (2) I don't eat it, for health reasons.
- (1) I eat it rarely.
- (0) Pass the ribs.

Heterosexism QUESTION #56

A close family member announces he or she is gay. What is your reaction?

- (3) I would give them a hug and commend their courage.
- (2) I would shake their hand and suggest support groups.
- (1) I would suggest therapy.
- (0) I would open the closet door and ask them to go back in.

QUESTION #57

Should Thanksgiving be a national holiday?

(3) No. To celebrate the genocide of Native Americans is obscene. To me, Thanksgiving is a day of mourning.

(2) Yes, but people should be reminded that Indians suffered under colonization.

(1) Yes. Thanksgiving is a joyous American tradition.

(0) Do you want dark meat or white?

QUESTION #58

Should Columbus Day be a national holiday?

(2) No. Christopher Columbus was an imperialist who raped and pillaged the original inhabitants of the New World. Furthermore, how could he "discover" a world that was already inhabited?

(1) Yes. Columbus's discovery of the New World was a major feat in world history.

(0) Yes—we need all the three-day weekends we can get.

Imperialism   QUESTION #59

How do you feel about the expansion of American fast-food restaurants and theme parks throughout the world?

(3)   It is wrong. Our country's cultural hegemony enforces a code of conformity that leads to worldwide homogenization.

(2)   I don't support it here, I don't support it there.

(1)   I say give the people what they want— that's the principle of supply and demand.

(0)   It's great. Now I have a reason to travel abroad.

Imperialism   QUESTION #60

How do you feel about U.S. intervention in Central American countries such as Panama and Grenada?

(3)   Read my bumper sticker: "U.S. Out of Central America."

(2)   We should send humanitarian aid to Central American countries that request it.

(1)   We must foster democracy and stop communism at any cost.

(0)   Colonize and make it official.

Is capital punishment an effective deterrent to crime?

(3) No, it is both inhumane and racist, since a disproportionate number of those executed are African-American men.

(2) There is no conclusive evidence.

(1) We'll never know until we adopt capital punishment in all fifty states with a Constitutional amendment.

(0) In the immortal words of Gary Gilmore: "Let's do it!"

You witness a drug deal. What do you do?

(3) I would form a community task force to patrol my neighborhood and offer drug counseling; after all, we need hugs, not drugs.

(2) I would anonymously inform the police if I was confident that the dealers and not the users would be caught.

(1) I would call the police and aid their investigation.

(0) Try to score.

A person attempts to mug you at gunpoint. What do you do?

(3) Although I disapprove of their violent methods, I understand that socioeconomic disadvantage can drive some people to crime; therefore, I would hand over my cash without resistance.

(2) I wouldn't want to get hurt, so I'd hand over the cash.

(1) If I felt I could overpower the mugger, I would try to; otherwise, I would reluctantly hand over the cash.

(0) Take target practice with my .357.

What is your opinion of gun control?

(3) We should outlaw all guns, including hunting weapons.

(2) We should outlaw handguns and assault weapons and extend the waiting period for purchases of all other guns.

(1) We should outlaw only semiautomatic assault weapons.

(0) You can find my opinion in the Constitution—the part about the right to bear arms.

Lookism   QUESTION #65

(Women only):
How do you feel about using cosmetics?

- (3) I never use them. The so-called beauty industry exploits animals, objectifies women, and promotes both ageism and lookism.
- (2) I use only cruelty-free neutral tones.
- (1) I like to wear make up and frankly think there are more important issues to discuss.
- (0) Tammy Faye Bakker is my role model.

Lookism   QUESTION #66

(Men only):
What is your image of the ideal woman?

- (3) I am attracted to people on the basis of their character, not their looks.
- (2) Although I try to avoid objectifying women, I do appreciate their beauty. Therefore, my ideal woman has both style and substance.
- (1) Miss America.
- (0) Miss November.

Lookism   QUESTION #67

(Women only):
Do you shave your legs and underarms?

> (3)   No. It is unnatural to alter one's body to conform to a definition of femininity created by a male-dominated society.
>
> (2)   I shave my lower legs and underarms in the summer; otherwise, I don't bother.
>
> (1)   Yes. It makes me look and feel more feminine.
>
> (0)   No. I have my entire body waxed on a regular basis.

Lookism   QUESTION #68

(Men only):
What would motivate you to exercise regularly?

> (3)   My belief in the theory of "sound mind, sound body."
>
> (2)   The need to offset unhealthy life choices, such as caffeine consumption and a sedentary desk job.
>
> (1)   It's a jungle out there and I want to make sure I can defend myself.
>
> (0)   To look buff and meet babes.

QUESTION #69

Should American military force be used beyond our borders to apprehend alleged violators of U.S. law?

(3) No. We have no right to intervene in the affairs of other countries, although, of course, the CIA does it all the time.

(3) No. I believe international law must supercede the mandate of the U.S. government.

(1) Yes, when the common interest of the American people is at stake.

(0) Kill 'em all and let God sort 'em out.

QUESTION #70

Should women in the armed forces engage in combat?

(3) No. Nobody should ever engage in combat.

(2) Yes. If women want to defend their country, they should have the right.

(1) No. Women are not physically suited for ground combat.

(0) No. They just want a legal excuse to kill men.

Militarism QUESTION #71

What role should the U.S. play in the New World Order?

- (3) To pay reparations to the victims of the Old World Order.
- (2) We should work together with the United Nations.
- (1) We should remain independent and isolated.
- (0) We are the New World Order.

Multiculturalism   QUESTION #72

Should college undergraduates be required to take a course in Western civilization?

    (3)   "Hey hey, ho ho, Western civ has got to go."

    (2)   No. Although these works are important, equal weight must given to non-Western perspectives.

    (1)   Yes. Western values are the cornerstone of modern society. If more people studied them, we would have a better-educated society.

    (0)   Yes—I already bought the Cliff's Notes.

Multiculturalism   QUESTION#73

Should college undergraduates be required to take a course in ethnic studies?

    (3)   Yes. It is long overdue. College curricula have perpetutated a male-dominated, Eurocentric worldview for too long. Ethnic studies would challenge this myth of cultural superiority.

    (2)   Yes. Colleges must reflect all elements of our multicultural society and teach people to become sensitive to differences.

    (1)   No. "Oppression studies" lowers academic standards by caving in to special interests and only creates divisiveness.

    (0)   "Hey hey, ho ho, ethnic studies has got to go."

Multiculturalism   QUESTION #74

Should our government support bilingual education?

    (2)   Absolutely. Enforcing a rigid code of linguistic conformity denies students' cultural identity and puts them at an academic disadvantage during the assimilation process.

    (1)   Why should the government pay for American children to be taught in a foreign language?

    (0)   If you can't talk English, you got no business being here.

Nationalism   QUESTION #75

If you were asked to serve in a war that you felt was unjust, what would you do?

    (3)   Set myself on fire in protest.

    (2)   Either go to jail or leave the country.

    (1)   My country right or wrong!

    (0)   I would follow the old saying: Join the armed forces, travel to exotic countries, meet interesting people, and kill them.

Nationalism   QUESTION #76

If someone set the flag on fire and you had no way to put it out other than to urinate on it, what would you do?

(3)   The question is sexist since it ignores the fact that women can't urinate in public as freely and easily as men.

(2)   The Bill of Rights guarantees free speech. Burning the flag is the ultimate test of that freedom, so I would not interfere.

(1)   People have died defending the flag and we should respect it; therefore, we should neither burn it nor urinate on it.

(0)   First, I would urinate on it. Then I would turn around and make sure to urinate all over the creep who set it on fire.

Nationalism   QUESTION #77

Should the national anthem be played before sporting and other entertainment events?

(3)   No. I think it promotes mindless jingoism—the kind that leads to wars.

(2)   No. We are a world of human beings, not nations; therefore, I don't recognize any national anthem, including our own.

(1)   Yes, it promotes patriotism and pride.

(0)   If I'm at a ballgame and I'm not out getting some hot dogs and beer, I always yell "wahoo!" after the part about "the land of the free."

Racism QUESTION #78

Are minority quotas necessary in hiring?

- (3) Yes. They are an absolute necessity if we are going to to redress the past and present evils of institutionalized racism.
- (2) Yes. It is not a perfect system, but without it minorities might never get hired.
- (1) No. I believe in meritocracy. Qualifications should be colorblind.
- (0) No. Just the opposite—thanks to reverse discrimination, we now need majority quotas.

Racism QUESTION #79

Should racial epithets and "inappropriately directed laughter" on college campuses result in punishment of the offenders?

- (3) Yes—freedom of expression is no more sacred than freedom from bigotry.
- (2) I do not condone hurtful behavior; however, I believe the mission of education is to enlighten, not punish.
- (1) Freedom of speech must apply to everyone, including bigots.
- (0) As long as it's not directed at me.

Racism QUESTION #80

If a Person of Color shops at an African-American-owned store to "support their own kind," are they committing a racist act?

- (3) No. Racism is power. People of Color have traditionally been denied power and, therefore, by definition, cannot be racists.
- (2) Yes. Everybody is a "recovering racist" and the sooner we realize that the sooner we can live in harmony.
- (1) Yes and it disturbs me that anyone would think otherwise.
- (0) No. It was better when all the races kept to themselves.

Sexism QUESTION #81

If a female employee is told by a male supervisor that she looks good, does that qualify as sexual harassment?

- (3) Yes. Engaging in lookism toward women is sexist, discriminatory, and, in the workplace, unlawful.
- (2) Whether it is sexual harassment depends on the situation; however, as a rule, comments about physical appearance in the workplace are inappropriate.
- (1) No. In the majority of cases it is probably well-intentioned and should be taken that way.
- (0) No. Women love to be flattered, whether they admit it or not.

Sexism   QUESTION #82

Could a woman be an effective president of the United States?

- (3) Absolutely. In fact, the United States would be a better place if we had a woman president.
- (2) Yes. Every candidate should be judged on his or her stands on the issues, not gender.
- (1) No—I doubt she could win a war.
- (0) No way—when her hormones started raging she might blow up the world.

Sexism   QUESTION #83

If a man asks a woman out to dinner, should he pay?

- (3) No. The myth of the "weaker sex" has disappeared—so should patronizing customs. The bill should be split between them.
- (2) It's up to the individuals involved. They should discuss it and reach a mutually satisfying agreement.
- (1) Yes. Call me old-fashioned but I think the concept of chivalry has merit.
- (0) Only if he's going to get something in return.

Wealth and Poverty   QUESTION #84

How should America solve its mounting financial problems?

- (3)   Tax the rich.
- (2)   A government bailout.
- (1)   Corporate grants and sponsorship.
- (0)   Tax the liberals.

Wealth and Poverty   QUESTION #85

Should we abolish the welfare system?

- (3)   No. The racist, capitalist system depends on exploiting a permanent underclass. The government should assist those who suffer under this inequitable system.
- (2)   No. The government has a responsibility to people in desperate need but should put more emphasis on job education.
- (1)   Yes. The system is a failure that just perpetuates the problems it was intended to solve.
- (0)   Yes. Why should my tax dollars support people watching soap operas while I put in an honest day's work?

Wealth and Poverty   QUESTION #86

Which of the following methods would be the best way to solve the unemployment issue?

(3)   Expand the scope of social services until we have achieved full employment.

(2)   Education and job programs.

(1)   Cut the welfare system and stop shipping jobs overseas.

(0)   Expand the NBA by 10,000 teams.

ARE YOU PC?

The final category of the quiz measures your level of commitment to PC causes. Again, a simple yes or no will do.

Are You PC?　　QUESTION #87

Do you volunteer any of your time to social services?

- (1)　Yes
- (0)　No

Are You PC?　　QUESTION #88

Do you boycott companies that sponsor conservative causes?

- (1)　Yes
- (0)　No

Are You PC?　　QUESTION #89

Have you ever boycotted certain produce such as lettuce or grapes to protest the growers' unfair labor practices?

- (1)　Yes
- (0)　No

Are You PC? QUESTION #90

Do you think political conflicts can be decided by nonviolent means?

    (1)   Yes
    (0)   No

Are You PC? QUESTION #91

Do you refuse to cross picket lines?

    (1)   Yes
    (0)   No

Are You PC? QUESTION #92

Do you think the convenience of human beings is more important than the protection of nature?

    (1)   No
    (0)   Yes

Are You PC? QUESTION #93

Do you think reverse discrimination is a real problem?

    (1)   No
    (0)   Yes

Are You PC? QUESTION #94

Do you think the media has a liberal bias?

    (1)   No
    (0)   Yes

Do you think the media has a right-wing bias?

   (1)   Yes
   (0)   No

Are You PC?　　QUESTION #96

Do you think the FBI has a file on you?

- (1)　Yes
- (0)　No

Are You PC?　　QUESTION #97

Is the word "empowered" a part of your daily vocabulary?

- (1)　Yes
- (0)　No

Are You PC?　　QUESTION #98

Do you use the word "fascist" to describe a person who uses their authority in a way you find offensive?

- (1)　Yes
- (0)　No

Are You PC?　　QUESTION #99

Do you use the term "differently sized" to describe people who are overweight?

- (1)　Yes
- (0)　No

Are you PC? QUESTION #100

Do you consider yourself PC?

- (3) No. I reject labels and suspect this term is being used as a tool of oppression.
- (2) Not really. I am sensitive to the issues but the term does not personally empower me.
- (1) No. I've been told that my political outlook is not particularly correct.
- (0) You must be kidding.

Are You PC? QUESTION #101

Do you experience PC-phobia (fear of not appearing politically correct)?

- (3) Never. I don't care what people think because I know I'm right.
- (2) Yes. I worry that others think I'm on "the wrong side" of issues that I am basically sympathetic to.
- (1) Yes. I don't enjoy being labeled a racist, sexist, homophobic pig just because I disagree with PC thinking.
- (0) Never. I don't care what people think because I know I'm right.

PC SCALE

POLITICALLY INCORRECT

0   Get a life—and please don't breed.

1–50   You qualify as a knee-jerk (yes, knee-jerk) conservative who probably believes the Communist menace is still lurking just around the corner, waiting to sap and impurify our precious bodily fluids.

51–75   Do you bounce checks on your favorite charity just for kicks? Well, even if you don't, you are either a borderline misanthrope or seriously dyspeptic. Lighten up.

76–100   You are too apathetic to look up the words like misanthrope and dyspeptic in the dictionary. Don't worry—you can go back to your TV set now and your couch potato ambition.

101–125   You are a silent but proud neocon-
servative; in other words, you
don't say what you think but you
probably enjoy thinking it. Most
likely, you can afford to remain
silent on the important social issues
of our time because you're sitting
on a big fat wallet.

126–150   You are a moderate. This means
while other people take stands, you
just wonder why everybody can't
be friends. Perhaps this explains
why you appear to agree with who-
ever you are with at the time.

POLITICALLY CORRECT

151–175   You are a cynic with a soft heart.
You don't like to be labeled, and
avoid being aligned with causes.
There may be some liberal views in
your closet, but they'll never be
outed.

176–200   You make a major effort to be toler-
ant of all points of view. You mean
well but still make an occasional
slip. In other words, you are a
prime candidate for a guilt com-
plex.

201–225   You are solidly PC. You are committed to positively impacting your environment and empowering others as you battle Western society's flawed values. The only question is: Do you consider yourself a realist or an idealist?

226–249   You qualify as a knee-jerk (yes, knee-jerk) PC person who probably doesn't see the humor in being called knee-jerk. Your PC credentials are truly impeccable. You practice what you preach and preach what you practice. One sermon you sometimes forget is that tolerance is not a one-way street.

250   Congratulations—it's not easy being perfect in an imperfect world, but you have done it. Write your own book (using recycled paper from naturally fallen trees) under the name of God because you are now officially holier-than-thou.

PC-SPEAK
GLOSSARY

Ableism: Bias against the physically challenged (see below)

Afrocentrism: A belief system based on the assumption that African culture is superior

Ageism: Bias against an individual based on their age

Animal companion: Pet

Cruelty-free products: Products that have not been tested on laboratory animals

Differently abled: See physically challenged

Differently sized: Overweight or undersized

Dolphin-safe tuna: Tuna fish caught without killing dolphins

Eurocentrism: A belief system based on the assumption that European culture is superior

Ethnocentrism: The belief that one's ethnic group is superior to others

Gynephobia: Fear of women

Handism: Bias against left-handed people

Heterosexism: Belief in heterosexuality as the definitive form of sexuality

Homophobia: Fear of and/or prejudice against homosexuals

Lookism: The practice of basing opinions on physical appearance

Mixed-hand usage: Ambidexterity

Multiculturalism: Study of all cultures as equally important

Outing: Revealing a person's sexual orientation without her/his consent

Ovulars: Seminars for womyn (see womyn)

People of Color: Non-Caucasians

Phallocentrism: Belief in the superiority of men

Physically challenged: Disabled

Pre-women: Teenage girls

Recovering racists: People who have realized they are racist and are in the process of reforming their attitudes

Scent-free environment: An event at which no one wears perfumes of any kind.

Self-segregation: A movement that stresses affirmation of one's own group identity before assimilation

Sizeism: Prejudice against the differently sized

Temporarily abled: Term to describe the non-physically challenged.

Temporarily young: Term to describe the not-yet-old

Womyn: Alternate spelling used to take the "men" out of "women"

SCORESHEET

Question	Score	Question	Score	Question	Score	Question	Score
1		26		51		76	
2		27		52		77	
3		28		53		78	
4		29		54		79	
5		30		55		80	
6		31		56		81	
7		32		57		82	
8		33		58		83	
9		34		59		84	
10		35		60		85	
11		36		61		86	
12		37		62		87	
13		38		63		88	
14		39		64		89	
15		40		65		90	
16		41		66		91	
17		42		67		92	
18		43		68		93	
19		44		69		94	
20		45		70		95	
21		46		71		96	
22		47		72		97	
23		48		73		98	
24		49		74		99	
25		50		75		100	
						101	
					TOTAL:		

SCORESHEET

Question	Score	Question	Score	Question	Score	Question	Score
1		26		51		76	
2		27		52		77	
3		28		53		78	
4		29		54		79	
5		30		55		80	
6		31		56		81	
7		32		57		82	
8		33		58		83	
9		34		59		84	
10		35		60		85	
11		36		61		86	
12		37		62		87	
13		38		63		88	
14		39		64		89	
15		40		65		90	
16		41		66		91	
17		42		67		92	
18		43		68		93	
19		44		69		94	
20		45		70		95	
21		46		71		96	
22		47		72		97	
23		48		73		98	
24		49		74		99	
25		50		75		100	
						101	
						TOTAL:	

SCORESHEET

Question	Score	Question	Score	Question	Score	Question	Score
1		26		51		76	
2		27		52		77	
3		28		53		78	
4		29		54		79	
5		30		55		80	
6		31		56		81	
7		32		57		82	
8		33		58		83	
9		34		59		84	
10		35		60		85	
11		36		61		86	
12		37		62		87	
13		38		63		88	
14		39		64		89	
15		40		65		90	
16		41		66		91	
17		42		67		92	
18		43		68		93	
19		44		69		94	
20		45		70		95	
21		46		71		96	
22		47		72		97	
23		48		73		98	
24		49		74		99	
25		50		75		100	
						101	
					TOTAL:		

SCORESHEET

Question	Score	Question	Score	Question	Score	Question	Score
1		26		51		76	
2		27		52		77	
3		28		53		78	
4		29		54		79	
· 5		30		55		80	
6		31		56		81	
7		32		57		82	
8		33		58		83	
9		34		59		84	
10		35		60		85	
11		36		61		86	
12		37		62		87	
13		38		63		88	
14		39		64		89	
15		40		65		90	
16		41		66		91	
17		42		67		92	
18		43		68		93	
19		44		69		94	
20		45		70		95	
21		46		71		96	
22		47		72		97	
23		48		73		98	
24		49		74		99	
25		50		75		100	
						101	
					TOTAL:		